the Country Friends™ Collection

Garden Fun

MARY ELIZABETH ··· loves her compost pile.

HOLLY ··· believes in organic gardening.

KATE ··· wonders if she could grow her own chocolate chips.

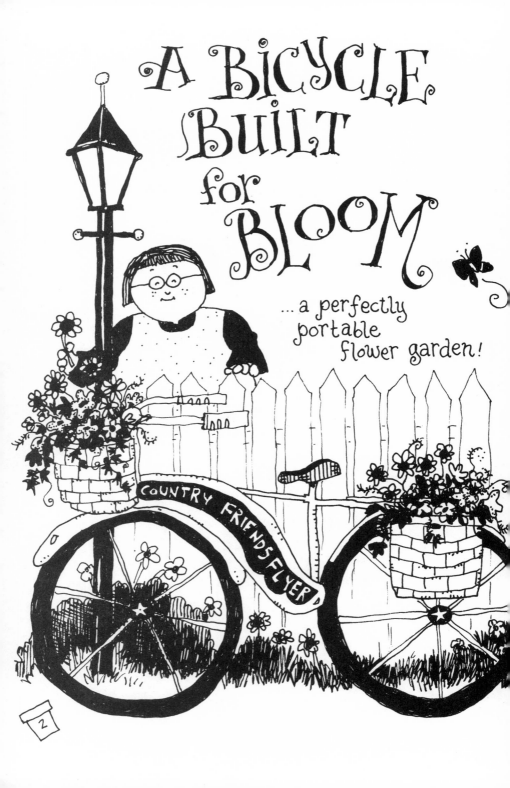

A BICYCLE BUILT for BLOOM

...a perfectly portable flower garden!

COUNTRY FRIENDS FLYER

2

Take one old-fashioned bike and add an inexpensive bicycle basket to the handlebars... and follow these steps:

1. **L**ine basket with mesh screen or spaghnum moss.

2. **F**ill basket three-fourths full of potting soil.

3. **P**lant with your favorite flowers... bright red geraniums, cascading petunias, ivy & pansies are nice.

MORE BLOOMING BIKE IDEAS

Add *streamers* to the handlebars for fun.

Tie on some *balloons* in bright colors for a birthday party.

Weave red, white & blue crepe paper through the tires' spokes on the Fourth of July. Tuck in some small flags, too, among the flowers in the basket.

DIG IN!

VEGGIE EXTRAVAGANZA

RADISHES

CARROTS

THE POTLUCK PARTY

with a vegetarian twist!

When? Where? Who?

When? Garden Harvest-Time

Where? In the Garden, of course!

Who? Your Country Friends™

I invite friends to bring a favorite dish using the bounty of the garden.

Holly's Veggie Picnic Packets

Make 'em ahead of time then toss 'em on the grill.

1 T. oil
1 T. white wine vinegar
1 T. white wine Worcestershire sauce
1 t. fresh tarragon, snipped or ¼ t. dried tarragon, crushed
¼ t. lemon peel, finely shredded
⅛ t. salt

12 large mushrooms, halved
2 small yellow summer squash, halved lengthwise & sliced
1 large onion, cut in chunks
1 stalk celery, chopped
1 small red pepper, sliced into strips

Make an 18" square by folding a 36" x 18" piece of heavy aluminum foil in half. In small bowl, combine oil, vinegar, Worcestershire sauce, tarragon, lemon peel & salt. Place veggies on foil. Fold up sides slightly ～ pour mixture over veggies. Finish folding edges to seal pouch securely. Grill on uncovered grill 30 minutes or 'til tender-crisp. Turn pouch occasionally for even cooking & to prevent burning.

Party in the Veggie Patch

Sippin' Tea

4 c. boiling water
5 to 6 regular teabags
½ c. sugar
4 c. tap water
juice of 1 lemon

Pour boiling water over teabags in heat-resistant pitcher. Steep 5 minutes. Remove teabags—don't squeeze! Stir in sugar 'til dissolved. Add water & juice. Cool, then serve over ice.

FRESH PRODUCE

Strangers are what Friends are made of. ~ Cullen Hightower
(Bring a friend to the party!)

... and YOU are Invited!

TASTY! Grandma's Scalloped Tomato Casserole

★

3·½ c. tomatoes, peeled & chopped
1 c. onions, chopped
½ c. cheese-flavored cracker crumbs
1·½ c. sugar
½ t. salt
8-oz. carton sour cream
1·½ c. seasoned croutons
1 T. butter, melted

★

Layer half each of tomatoes, onions, cracker crumbs, sugar & salt in buttered 1·½-quart casserole dish. Repeat layers. Bake 20 minutes at 325°. Remove from oven ~ spread sour cream on top. Sprinkle with croutons. Drizzle melted butter over top of croutons. Bake for 10 minutes more. Serves 6.

Kate's SPICY CORN on the COB ... Woo·eee!

Serve fresh, hot corn on the cob with this zippy embellishment:

½ c. butter, softened
1 jalapeño pepper, seeded & minced
1 t. chili powder

Combine all ingredients & mix well.

★

Garden Glories:
Holly's Centerpieces for a garden Party

Use clean empty tin cans with bright veggie labels to hold simple bouquets of black-eyed susans, zinnias, daisies & other cutting flowers. Line 'em up down the center of your table!

PEA   CARR   TOMA

Clay pots full of colorful vegetables look stunning on the table ∽ turn some pots on their sides and let the veggies spill out. Flowering kale looks especially beautiful in different-sized pots.

More garden party ideas for a glorious time!

Set your table with a festive plaid cloth, or try your hand at decorating a white tablecloth with veggie prints: simply cut a vegetable in half, dip it into fabric paint and stamp a design!

Buy garden gloves and tuck the silverware inside one at each place setting... add a bandana for a napkin in the glove, too.

Serve pasta, fresh veggie salads & other foods in garden buckets; use new hand-shovels for serving tools!

Hollowed-out potatoes, squash & peppers make clever votive candleholders to set at each place.

garden wagon

Get out your trusty red wagon or wheelbarrow for a portable party express: fill with ice, glasses & drinks ∼ and don't forget the handshovel for an ice scoop!

Sunny 'brellas

I pledge allegiance to the flag of the Un...

YOU NEED:

* A canvas umbrella (open-weave, non-fabric ones will not work!)
* Assorted fabric scraps
* Jumbo rick-rack, ribbon, fringe & trims
* Fabric paints
* Brushes
* Stencils
* Fabric glue
* Iron-on fusible webbing, in sheets & tape
* Silk flowers
* Buttons
* what-have-you

put your imagination to work! Cut out fabric shapes & glue on, trim your umbrella with buttons & fabric paints, stencil a checkerboard edge... just have fun!

BRIGHT 'BRELLA Ideas

STARS & STRIPES
(JUST LIKE MARY ELIZABETH's!)

Use fusible webbing to iron small fabric flags from the craft store to your umbrella. Add hand-drawn red, white & blue fabric paint stars and a patriotic message.

SUNSHINE & MOONSHINE

Use gold & silver fabric paints to make your old umbrella glow... in fact, why not add glow-in-the-dark painted stars for a night-time shine?

SECRET GARDEN 'BRELLA

Stencil a green leafy vine all around the edge, then glue on all kinds of silk flower blossoms for a bloomin' new look.

To love and be loved is to feel the sun from both sides. — DAVID VISCOTT

Celebrate the first HOT summer day: Sit on the grass in your garden under your sunny 'brella and sip something cool... how about lemonade with strawberries frozen into the ice cubes? A real treat!

ALL★AMERICAN

PUT THE KIDS TO WORK GATHERING STICKS OF ALL SIZES, THEN TRY SOME COUNTRY FRIENDS™ CRAFT IDEAS FOR THE GARDEN:

WELCOME

★ TWIGS MAKE FUN BORDERS & LETTERS ON GARDEN SIGNS.

★ DRILL HOLES IN YOUR PUMPKIN-HEADS THIS FALL & MAKE TWIG HAIR-DOS!

The trash and litter of nature disappears into the ground with the passing of each year, but man's litter has more permanence.
— JOHN STEINBECK

STICK ROUND*UP

★ BUILD A SIMPLE TRELLIS BY TYING SMALLER STICKS TO LONG ANCHOR TWIGS.

★ ADD TWIGS TO A GARDEN FENCE OR GATE FOR VISUAL INTEREST.

Now is no time to think of what you do not have. Think of what you can do with what there is. — ERNEST HEMINGWAY

STicKs

continued:

★ BIND
TOGETHER
A FAT
BUNDLE OF
STURDY
STICKS
& MOUNT
A PUMPKIN
ON
TOP
FOR
A
UNIQUE
FALL
TOPIARY.

★ FILL A WINDOWBOX WITH GOURDS,
LEAVES & TWIGS... NATURE'S BEAUTY!

★ MAKE TWIGGY BLINDS FOR YOUR WINDOWS
(above) BY SELECTING TWO FAIRLY GOOD-
SIZED STICKS & NAILING OR TYING TWIGS
ACROSS THEM.

★ SEND THE KIDS OUT ON AN ALPHABET TWIG HUNT:
FIND STICKS THAT LOOK LIKE THE LETTERS OF
THEIR NAMES, THEN HELP THEM MOUNT THE
TWIGS ON A PAINTED BOARD... FUN!

14

KIDS' Mystery Garden

OPEN SEVERAL PACKAGES OF FLOWER SEEDS, AND SAVE THE PACKETS. THEN... PREPARE YOUR PLANTING AREA AND GET PLANTIN'!

PLAN **A** DUMP ALL DIFFERENT KINDS OF SEEDS TOGETHER, THEN SCATTER THE MIX OVER PREPARED GROUND—RAKE GENTLY 'TIL JUST COVERED WITH SOIL. GUESS WHAT'S WHAT AS YOUR MYSTERY GARDEN BLOOMS!

OR AN-EASIER-TO-SOLVE GARDEN PUZZLE:

PLAN **B** KEEP DIFFERENT SEEDS IN DIFFERENT ROWS—DAISIES IN ONE, MARIGOLDS IN THE NEXT, AND SO ON. AS FLOWERS BLOOM, PULL OUT THE SEED PACKETS & START GUESSING!

Never a daisy grows but a mystery guides the growing. —RICHARD REALF

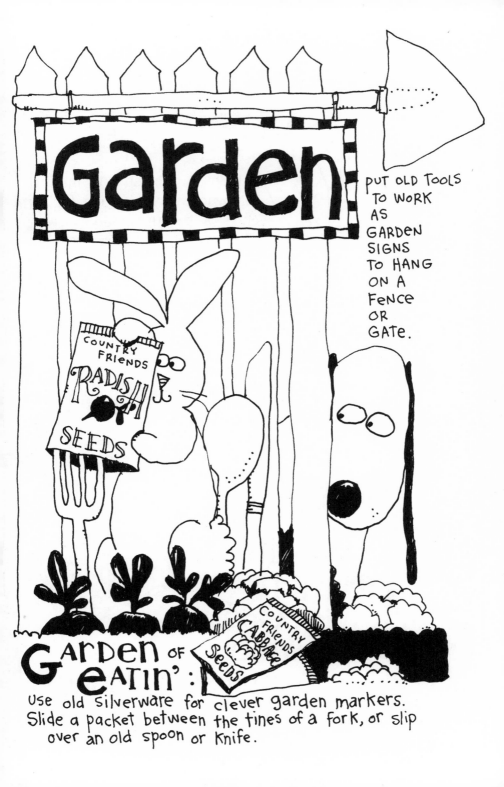

Garden

PUT OLD TOOLS TO WORK AS GARDEN SIGNS TO HANG ON A FENCE OR GATE.

COUNTRY FRIENDS RADISH SEEDS

COUNTRY FRIENDS CABBAGE SEEDS

GARDEN OF EATIN':

Use old silverware for clever garden markers. Slide a packet between the tines of a fork, or slip over an old spoon or knife.

GARDEN SIGN IdeaS

Grab an old board, some paint & a brush and make a whimsical wooden sign for gate, fence or potting shed!

I Love Gardens a WholeBunch

Welcome Birdies

Plant a little Sunshine

Secret garden

All American Garden

Other ideas for signs...

* Listen.
* Come play in my garden.
* Walk with God in the garden.
* Gather friends like flowers.
* No Weeds allowed!

more GARDEN Decoration (as if flowers aren't enough!)

Scout around at yard sales for old garden gates made of wooden pickets or wrought iron... even chain link! "Plant" it in your garden with tall flowers behind it and short, colorful beds in front, and decorate your gate with tools, signs, hats, flags... a little architectural interest in your flower bed will wake it up!

Bring home a pretty hand-chosen Rock from each trip to the beach or river.... a memory to keep in your garden.

*The sky is the daily bread of the eyes. —RALPH WALDO EMERSON

* One touch of nature makes the whole world kin. — SHAKESPEARE

* More than anything, I must have flowers, always, always. — CLAUDE MONET

The

BRAIDED
MOP HAIR
SHOVEL HEAD
BANDANA
OLD JEWELRY
GINGHAM
SHIRT
HOMESPUN
JUMPER
APPLIQUÉD
FLAG
POCKETS
SILVER-
WARE HANDS
POLKA-DOTTED
APRON
BOOTS

20

Remember that the most beautiful things in the world are
the most useless; peacocks and lilies for instance.
- JoHN Ruskin -

Well-Dressed Scarecrow

She can't just wear any old thing... or can she? Have a garden party and ask each guest to bring something for your garden guardian ... just remember, no high heels allowed in the veggie patch!

FASHION STATEMENTS AMONG THE RUTABAGAS:

RECYCLE A BIG OLD CAN FOR THE SCARECROW HEAD... OR USE A PUMPKIN!

AN OLD PAN MAKES A SNAZZY HAT ON A TIN-PAN NOGGIN

SAVE YOUR WORN-OUT JAMMIES & NIGHTIES FOR HER EVENING WEAR!

Zest is the secret of all beauty.
— CHRISTIAN DIOR

BANNERS

KATE LAND

WELCOME TO KATE COUNTRY!
NO DOUBT WHOSE GARDEN YOU'RE IN. MAKE YOUR OWN TERRITORIAL FLAG! USE FABRIC PAIN

HOLLY'S SUNSHINE SIGN
...BRIGHTENS UP THE CLOUDIEST DAY!

A BRIGHT YELLOW-&-WHITE-STRIPED CANVAS FLAG SHINES WITH A GOLD SUN; RED STAR-SHAPED SEQUINS GIVE A SUN-SHINY RAY OF CHEER-YOU-UP SHIMMER. FLY IT HIGH OVER A BED OF YELLOW BLOSSOMS!

FLOWERS

FLY-AWAY-HOME BANNER

WHEN YOU SEE THAT LIGHT, BRIGHT RED LADYBUG FLAG, YOU'LL KNOW YOU'RE HOME. WHITE BACKGROUND WITH FABRIC-PAINTED POLKA-DOTS REALLY SHOWS OFF THE LADYE WITH HER SEWN-ON WHITE BUTTON SPOTS!

22

We are not sent into this world to do anything into which we cannot put our hearts.
—JOHN RUSKIN—

AND FLAGS

...EASY TO MAKE!

HERE'S WHAT YOU NEED:

- ▲ FABRIC DESIGNED FOR OUTDOOR BANNERS & FLAGS
- ▲ MATCHING THREAD
- ▲ FUSIBLE IRON-ON WEBBING WITH PAPER BACKING
- ▲ FABRIC PAINTS

HERE'S HOW TO:

1. FOLD OVER EDGES OF FABRIC ON THREE SIDES — STITCH.

2. FOLD OVER TOP EDGE & STITCH, LEAVING AN OPENING WIDE ENOUGH FOR A POLE.

3. CUT OUT DESIGN ELEMENTS ON DESIRED FABRICS. TRACE DESIGN ON PAPER SIDE OF FUSIBLE WEBBING ~ CUT IT OUT, TOO.

4. IRON ONTO FLAG, THEN STITCH DESIGN DOWN.

5. ADD DETAILS & ACCENTS TO YOUR FLAG WITH FABRIC PAINTS... LET DRY.

6. SLIP IT ON A POLE OR LONG STURDY STICK!

Cozy Corners

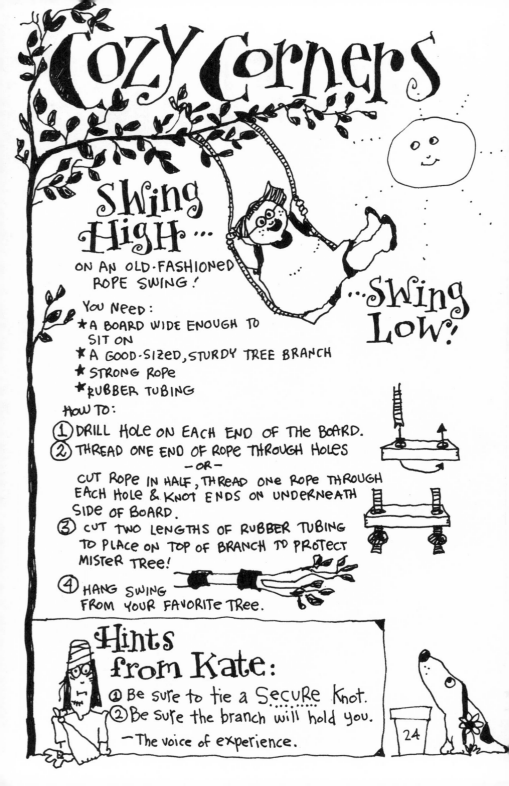

Swing High...

ON AN OLD-FASHIONED ROPE SWING!

You Need:
* A BOARD WIDE ENOUGH TO SIT ON
* A GOOD-SIZED, STURDY TREE BRANCH
* STRONG ROPE
* RUBBER TUBING

How To:
1. DRILL HOLE ON EACH END OF THE BOARD.
2. THREAD ONE END OF ROPE THROUGH HOLES
   — OR —
   CUT ROPE IN HALF, THREAD ONE ROPE THROUGH EACH HOLE & KNOT ENDS ON UNDERNEATH SIDE OF BOARD.
3. CUT TWO LENGTHS OF RUBBER TUBING TO PLACE ON TOP OF BRANCH TO PROTECT MISTER TREE!
4. HANG SWING FROM YOUR FAVORITE TREE.

...Swing Low!

Hints from Kate:
1. Be sure to tie a SECURE knot.
2. Be sure the branch will hold you.

— The voice of experience.

24

Just BIG Enough For Me (and You!)

Twiggy Hide·aways

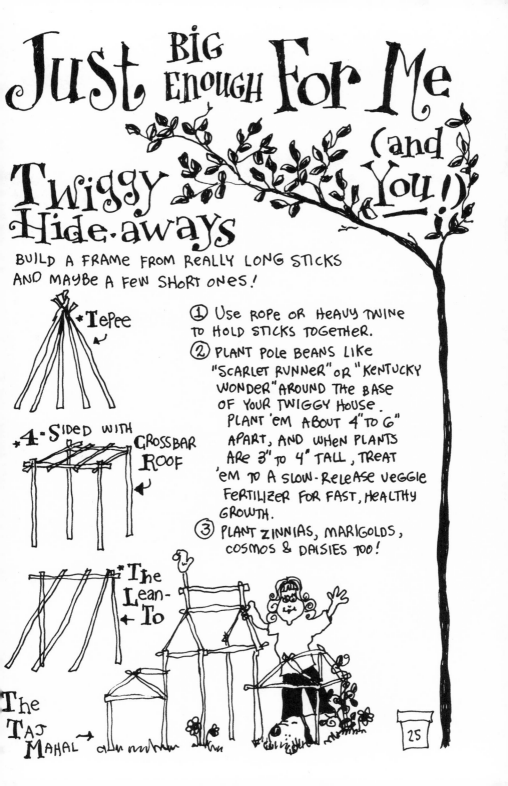

BUILD A FRAME FROM REALLY LONG STICKS
AND MAYBE A FEW SHORT ONES!

*Tepee

*4-SIDED WITH CROSSBAR ROOF

*The Lean-To

The TAJ MAHAL →

① Use ROPE OR HEAVY TWINE TO HOLD STICKS TOGETHER.

② PLANT POLE BEANS LIKE "SCARLET RUNNER" OR "KENTUCKY WONDER" AROUND THE BASE OF YOUR TWIGGY HOUSE.
PLANT 'EM ABOUT 4" TO 6" APART, AND WHEN PLANTS ARE 3" TO 4" TALL, TREAT 'EM TO A SLOW-RELEASE VEGGIE FERTILIZER FOR FAST, HEALTHY GROWTH.

③ PLANT ZINNIAS, MARIGOLDS, COSMOS & DAISIES TOO!

25

Hanging Out in the Hammock

Here's the best of summer recipes,
all you needs a hammock and
two trees~
the perfect way to spend an hour
in your own private, shady bower:

Start with softly blowing breeze,
add chirp of birds and buzz of bees
pour in a glass of something cool
and no interruptions ~ that's a rule;

Put a pillow under head,
nap outdoors instead of bed
The soft, sweet scent of grass & daisy
will make you feel oh-so-lazy
as you softly swing away
the better part of a summer day!

CLAY POT Twinklers

...So pretty!

Hang a string of our twinklers in the trees or on the porch for perfect garden party lights.

You'll Need:

* Strand of twinkle lights
* 2" clay pots ~ one for each light bulb on strand
* Drill with ½"- drill bit

How To:

Make a hole in bottom of clay pots using drill. Remove light bulb from light fixture on strand. Place fixture into hole from outside of pot ~ replace bulb inside the pot. (If needed, enlarge hole by scraping edge with an old sharp knife or sandpaper. Light should fit snugly.)

A garden must be looked into, and dressed as a body. — George Herbert

Come On!
DOWN the GARDEN PATH

HI

Molly age 5

secret garden

YOU WILL NEED:

* ITEMS FOR MOLDS— CARDBOARD PIECES & MASKING TAPE OR PLASTIC LINERS FROM FLOWERPOT SAUCERS
* CONCRETE MIX— QUICK-SETTING KIND
* PLASTIC BUCKET FOR MIXING
* WATER
* MEASURING CUP
* PENCIL
* ROCKS, BROKEN CERAMIC PIECES, MARBLES, SHELLS OR COLORED BEADS
* PLASTIC GLOVES FOR HAND IMPRINTS

1. FIRST THINGS FIRST: <u>PLAN</u> YOUR DESIGN! IT'S BEST TO MAKE IT ON PAPER FIRST.

2. <u>FIGURE OUT</u> YOUR <u>MOLD</u>. DESIGN YOUR OWN SHAPE USING CARDBOARD PIECES & MASKING TAPE ~ FOR EXAMPLE, TO MAKE A HEART-SHAPE, CUT 2" STRIPS OF CARDBOARD. ON LARGE FLAT PIECE, DRAW HEART DESIGN. BEND CARDBOARD STRIPS TO FIT SIDES & TAPE INTO PLACE. SEAL EDGES WELL SO CONCRETE DOESN'T LEAK OUT! OR YOU CAN <u>SIMPLY USE PLASTIC FLOWERPOT LINERS</u> FOR NICE ROUND STEPPING STONES.

QUICK SET CONC

28

Customized Stepping Stones for your garden

3. USE BUCKET TO PREPARE CONCRETE; FOLLOW INSTRUCTIONS FOR MIXING ON PACKAGE. POUR INTO MOLD 'TIL MIXTURE IS EVEN WITH TOP EDGE. SMOOTH THE SURFACE.

4. CREATE YOUR DESIGN! USE PENCIL TO ETCH LETTERS & DESIGNS INTO CONCRETE. FIRMLY IMPLANT STONES & OTHER OBJECTS INTO CONCRETE SO THEY DON'T LOOSEN & FALL OUT. FOR HAND PRINTS, BE SURE & WEAR PLASTIC GLOVES.

5. LET STONE DRY FOR SEVERAL DAYS TO LET CONCRETE CURE WELL BEFORE YOU PLACE IT ON THE GROUND.

6. REMOVE STONE FROM MOLD BY REMOVING CARDBOARD SIDES OR BY GENTLY PEELING MOLD FROM STONE.

7. PUT YOUR NEW STEPPING STONE ON PATHWAY SO IT IS FLUSH WITH THE GROUND.

HOLLY'S garden

SPOT DOG

est. 1998

welcome country friends

QUICK SET concrete

NOTHING IS MORE COMPLETELY THE CHILD OF ART THAN A GARDEN. — WALTER SCOTT

Holly's **Ideas** for **Stepping Stones**

Try a different shape ～ star, oval, square, fish, bugs, flowers, crescent moon... be original!

Make miniature stepping stones for a fairy garden, or to edge a flower garden.

Use pizza boxes to make big square stones!

Stones make great gifts! Let the kids make a set for Granny's garden path.

I have never had so many good ideas day after day as when I worked in the garden. ～ John Erskine

Hey! Can one imbed chocolate chip cookies in concrete?

Kate's easy Ham and Cheese Salad

...perfect after a long hot day in the dirt!

YUM

8-oz. pkg. corkscrew pasta
½ lb. cooked HAM, cut in Julienne strips
1 c. small broccoli flowerets
1 c. frozen green peas, thawed
1 small yellow summer squash, sliced thin
1 small sweet red pepper, thinly sliced
4 oz. Swiss cheese, cubed
½ c. mayonnaise
¼ c. Dijon mustard
¼ c. milk
¼ c. parmesan cheese, grated

Prepare pasta according to package. Drain. Rinse with cold water — drain again. Combine macaroni & veggies in mixing bowl. Prepare dressing by mixing together mayonnaise, mustard & milk. Pour over pasta & veggies. Toss gently, and sprinkle with parmesan cheese. Chill at least 2 hours. Serves 6.

Just Peachy FACE TREAT

After a sunny day pulling weeds, try this sweet skin moisturizer:

Blend together in a blender or food processor one peach & just enough heavy cream to make a nice "spread". Massage into skin. Resist urge to EAT face cream.

It's a good kind of tired.

All is miracle.

The stupendous order of nature, the revolution of a hundred millions of worlds around a million of suns, the activity of light, the life of animals, **all are grand and perpetual miracles.**

—Voltaire—